T5-CVF-042

GLOW IN THE DARK STICKER BOOK

How to use this book

Read the captions, then find the
sticker that best fits the space.
(Hint: check the sticker labels for clues!)

•

Charge your stickers under a bright light or
in the sunshine to ensure they glow.

•

There are lots of fantastic
extra stickers, too!

Penguin Random House

Writer and Editor Frankie Hallam
Art Editor Jon Hall
Designer Vicky Read
Senior Pre-Production Producer Jennifer Murray
Senior Producer Mary Slater
Managing Editor Emma Grange
Managing Art Editor Vicky Short
Publishing Director Mark Searle

First American Edition, 2024
Published in the United States by DK Publishing
1745 Broadway, 20th Floor, New York, NY 10019

Page design copyright © 2024 Dorling Kindersley Limited
DK, a Division of Penguin Random House LLC
24 25 26 27 28 10 9 8 7 6 5 4 3 2
002–339521–Mar/2024

A catalog record for this book is available from the Library of Congress.
ISBN 978-0-7440-9376-6

DK books are available at special discounts when purchased in
bulk for sales promotions, premiums, fund-raising, or educational
use. For details, contact: DK Publishing Special Markets,
1745 Broadway, 20th Floor, New York, NY 10019
SpecialSales@dk.com

Printed and bound in China

www.dk.com

MIX
Paper | Supporting
responsible forestry
FSC™ C018179

This book was made with Forest
Stewardship Council™ certified
paper - one small step in DK's
commitment to a sustainable future.
For more information go to
www.dk.com/our-green-pledge

MEET TEAM SPIDEY

Here's a team that's great in a sticky situation! Your Friendly Neighbourhood Spiders know that teamwork is the best way to get things done. Whether they're Web-Slinging with their amazing friends or putting a stop to their fearsome foes, they always do their best—and have fun too! GO-WEBS-GO!

SPIDEY
When Peter Parker was bitten by a radioactive spider, he became Spider-Man! Spidey always looks out for his team. He knows trouble is coming when his Spidey-Sense tingles.

SPIN
Spin is Spidey's best friend. He has many incredible powers, such as an Arachno-Sting that he uses to put villains to sleep if they're causing trouble.

GHOST-SPIDER
When Gwen Stacy puts on her suit she becomes Ghost-Spider! This super-cool Super Hero is the detective of Team Spidey—and she's a wizard on the drums, too!

GHOST-SPIDER'S POWERS
Ghosty has awesome web-wings under her arms that can help her glide through the air. She's always there to help her friends.

SPIDEY'S POWERS
Peter uses his powers of invention to create glowing webs, and Team Spidey uses them to light the way through New York City at night. GLOW-WEBS-GLOW!

SPIN'S POWERS
When Spin isn't glowing up, he can turn invisible with his amazing cloaking abilities. The Spiders would be lost without Spin, even if they can't always see him!

WEBBED-WONDERS
Spidey to the Power of 3! When things get darkest, Team Spidey glows the brightest. Teamwork makes the Spiders shine!

AMAZING FRIENDS

The members of Team Spidey aren't afraid to ask for help when they need it. Their friends are never far away and always have their backs. These spectacular heroes each have their own special powers, but when they use them together they become an unstoppable team!

REPTIL

Reptil helped Miles stop Green Goblin from destroying a dinosaur exhibition at the museum. He used his powers to turn into a pterodactyl!

WASP

Where Wasp finds a problem, she is there with a tiny-size solution. Wasp and Ant-Man make a great team, and she's not afraid to tell villains to buzz off.

IT'S SPIDEY TIME!

Stopping bad guys and crawling walls—Team Spidey does it all! It's tough being a Super Hero sometimes, but it's much easier with great friends to help out.

HULK

This green giant is a friendly one, but he can often lose his temper! Sometimes Hulk doesn't know his own strength, but his heart is always in the right place.

BLACK PANTHER

Black Panther comes from the African nation of Wakanda. His special suit is made of vibranium, the strongest metal in the world.

ANT-MAN

When you need someone small, Ant-Man is the hero to call. He has the power to shrink down to the size of an insect and can also grow into a giant.

IRON MAN

Tony Stark is always there when the Web-Slingers need him. This world-famous Super Hero is part of another incredible team that you might know—the Avengers!

MS. MARVEL

When Kamala Khan becomes Ms. Marvel, she turns into a super-stretchy Super Hero. She once helped Spidey round up some mischievous monkeys that had escaped from the zoo!

FEARSOME FOES

These villains love to cause trouble—the more destructive the better! Team Spidey has to work together to put a stop to them. That's why the Spiders and their friends will always win the day—they look out for each other! Which villain do you think is the most naughty?

ELECTRO

Electro has the amazing power of electricity. If only she would use it for good! It's no shock that this villain keeps trying to steal all of the city's energy for herself.

GREEN GOBLIN

When the Spiders hear Green Goblin's glider in the sky, they have to be alert. Gobby is always scheming and can't be trusted!

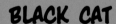

BLACK CAT

Pretty things are Black Cat's weakness. She once took an egg from a beautiful bird in the city zoo! Team Spidey returned it to mama bird in one piece.

RHINO

Rhino's on a rampage! This stomping super-villain is always stealing things and will stop at nothing to get what he wants.

SANDMAN

Sandman is able to turn his whole body into sand within seconds. This villain is always ruining everybody's fun. His specialty is destroying sandcastles on the beach!

DOC OCK

One of the smartest villains in town, Doc Ock is always inventing things to try to take over the city. She once used an invention to shrink Team Spidey to the size of ants!

SUPER VILLAINS

These tiresome tricksters won't give Team Spidey a day's rest. They are always trying to spoil things and think only about themselves. Team Spidey has had enough!

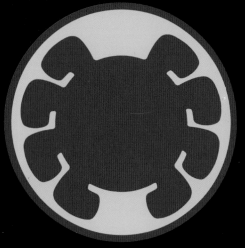

TERRIFIC TECHNOLOGY

Welcome to WEB-Quarters HQ, where all of Team Spidey's technology is created. The star of this hidden hideout is WEB-Ster, a supercomputer that helps to solve crimes and save the day! Team Spidey's machines are not always what they seem. Some can even climb up walls, just like the Spiders!

WEB-QUARTERS
This secret building is hidden under Peter's backyard! Not even Peter's Aunt May knows that it's there. Team Spidey meets here to figure out its next moves.

GHOST-COPTER
Each Spider has their own vehicle to help them speed things up. This super-fast Ghost-Copter helps Ghosty to spot trouble from the sky.

TWIST-E
Meet Twist-E, Miles's spider-bot! This metal mischief-maker is a good buddy to Miles. He teaches Twist-E to do cool tricks, fly, and spin around, just like Miles!